The Past Isn't Done with Me Yet

The Past Isn't Done with Me Yet

Poems by

Denise Sedman

Cover image by Diane DeCillis.
Author photo by Dakota Roos, Sunflower Productions.
Cover design by Shay Culligan

ISBN: 978-1-63980-417-7

Kelsay Books
502 South 1040 East, A-119
American Fork, Utah 84003
Kelsaybooks.com

To my family, Boyd Smith, Aaron Sedman, Joyce Urbanczyk

To my friends and mentors, M.L. Liebler, Diane DeCillis, Russ Thorburn, Linda Sienkiewicz . . . and the incredible poetry chick Pat Kearney (RIP)

About This Book

This book, *The Past Isn't Done With Me Yet,* is dedicated to those who have experienced abuse and/or depression. Know that you are seen. If your family didn't talk about abuse, this book will reveal the unspoken.

If you haven't personally experienced abuse and/or bipolar depression, you can learn more about the cycle. We're not alone in our journey for peace. Speak up!

Acknowledgments

Thank you to the following publications, where versions of these poems previously appeared:

Abandon Automobile: "These Words Will Not Change"

New Verse News: "Farm Aid"

Panoply: "My Choice"

Peninsula Poets: "An Exacto Knife and a Photo Album," "These Words Will Not Change," "Up in Smoke"

Poets Reading the News: "Forgiveness: A Daughter's Story," "The Human Condition"

Praycha Review: "Under the Influence of Depression"

Westland Writes: "Remnants"

Contents

Remnants

I saw his death suit
in the closet
with a pair of

red socks
in the breast
pocket of his jacket.

I'd never see
those red socks
inside his coffin.

He had a certain
destiny, which
was in Hell.

I prayed
the Devil
would let him in.

Now he's a spirit
swaddled in
a satin sea.

One velvet rose,
full of thorns,
punctures him.

His cycle is complete.
I believe I'm done with
my past.

But why
isn't the past
done with me?

Dirty Hands

What comes from dirt
goes back to dirt.
It's nature's way
of reminding us
life is not forever.

What dirt in your soul
could no Rosary expunge?
Even seven Hail Marys
cannot forgive you.

The Blue Marble

My sister steals a blue marble
from a Chinese Checkers' game,
glues it onto her Popsicle-stick box,

makes one-word-slips of paper,
tears them to pieces,
stuffs better daydreams inside.

No one cares, so she mumbles to herself,
makes a gimp for her sister,
watches soap operas all day.

He told her don't open closed doors.
Yet she twists the knob and says,
"I'm going to kill myself."

He says, "I don't give a shit.
Kill yourself. Get the hell out
of here." I'm not sure how

the knife gets back into the drawer
before she shimmies next to me,
but I die one hundred deaths, waiting.

These Women Are Me

At 79, Aunt Nancy could still swing a pipe.
In fact, she broke her neighbor's wrist
slapping at it like she was meshugana.

She got Tasered by the police
when she resisted arrest.

They threw her in jail,
told her to stop drinking hater-aid
and said she should be ashamed.

Her behavior was no surprise to me
because I come from a strong line of women
who have violence in their veins.

I remember when my mother
burned a hole in my hand.
She asked me to watch
smoke come from her ears.

I put my hand on her heart,
like she told me,
watched her puff
a drag from her cigarette,
looked at her ears,
and then bam!

Like a cartoon character, I was on fire.
These women want me to take their hate.

The Human Condition

RIP Anthony Bourdain
June 25, 1956 to June 8, 2018

It's all about blood, organs, cruelty and decay;
danger, risking the dark, going to bed
with sweats, chills and vomits.

He wanted it all:
the cuts and burns on his hands and wrists,
ghoulish kitchen humor, the free food,
harsh nerve-shattering chaos;
the sheer weirdness of kitchen life;
a last stop for misfits,

the dreamers, crackpots, refugees,
and sociopaths; roasting bones,
searing fish, and simmering liquids;
the noise and clatter, the hiss and spray,
flames, smoke and steam, he said
it's a life that grinds you down,

you'd think chefs would kill one another;
jam a boning knife into another cook's ribs,
or hit his brain with a meat mallet.
Instead, Bourdain chose to dry age.

—Erasure poem from Anthony Bourdain's article in *The New Yorker,* April 19,
1999, "Don't Eat Before Reading This."

Farm Aid

Cows have been milked
and chickens fed.

Daddy's awake since
before a light's been
switched on Wall Street,

All this talk about commodities.
Finances flopping,
unmanageable stress.

I heard the neighbor tied a rope
on a beam in the barn.
Hanged himself.

He tried the suicide hotline,
but the phone rang off the hook.

He Said . . .

It didn't happen
when there was a tsunami
in the Indian Ocean

Waves went above 40 feet
as this uncontrollable disaster
became your wake of devastation

Then you peed your pants
became rigid, disconnected
readied for an institution

He prays you'll recover forever
but it'll happen again
you have no choice

Signals

When I tell you
I have bipolar disorder,
you move away from me,
glance at my pockets,
wonder if I've got a .45 inside.
Crane to look at my wrists,
squint for a scar or
a semi-colon tattoo,
the ink says my story goes on.

#MeToo

His roommate stayed silent
to my screams of "no . . ."

I never told anyone
Why would I?

It happened to my mother
They called her a whore

I knocked down a lamp
when he pulled down my jeans
just enough for his satisfaction

I didn't tell my mother
Why would I?

When my dad tried it
she didn't respond,
not even a flinch.

Silence cannot endure

#MeToo

Last to Go

The thought of that purple bike
still makes me cringe—
banana seat, its squat frame
just like yours. And your diamond?

A wedding ring handed
down like a rotten marriage.
It still pinches my finger.

Those gifts weren't exactly
what I wanted when I was sixteen.
Dear mother, it's not enough.
I can't bury you in peace.

It's Dad's knuckle-ready fists,
jabbing like boxing gloves,
meeting my jaw that gave me
purple bruises, a cut lip
and a broken ear drum.

Mother, you saw it happen
and just like now, you
can't speak, but please
take my screams with you.
The hearing is the last to go.

Up in Smoke

You stroke your hair, gone white from sassy red.
It hurts too much to put color in anymore,
The cancerous tumor will be the death of you.
The curse, the cause of your pain.
But you look so peaceful, lying in bed.
One less day, shriveling as the daylight dims.
You smoked three packs of cigarettes a day so
it's no surprise that you have your pretend smokes.

The long drags, the pauses, the elegant hand gestures,
your lips holding your killer steady, puff then exhale;
you wouldn't change your habits now.
The doctor said, it's too late. You have six months
to live. He suggests you *put your house in order,*
as if you could get your house out of its own mess.

The House on Lumpkin Street

In the bathroom,
tiny ceramic tiles
loosen from their hold,
bulge from heavy weight
that burdens their existence.

Because they cannot
hold themselves together,
the father uses a trowel,

spreading cold cement,
to make a patch.

       My unbreakable river of gray,
       you were silenced by a rug.

1970 Blue Comet

When I hear the crashing noise,
it sounds like two tin pots and pans
banging together. The steel pole
does not care. It stands like a
fearless superman while
my car is dented, both
bumper and trunk.

The blow makes the trunk look like
ass cheeks puckering up, waiting
for a dent remover to make it right.

When my father hits me, it's
no accident. He takes pleasure punching
on the accelerator, grabbing my neck.
With one grip, my head hits the wall.

Forgiveness

(A daughter's story)

It's October in my kitchen,
I bless your card,
lick the envelope's bitter glue:

Dear Dad,
Have a wonderful birthday.
Love, Your daughter.

I squeeze niceness out of a blue pen,
wring pain out of my palms.
Why doesn't Hallmark
have a dysfunctional daddy series?

I'm sending a card
to a father who isn't worth
the time it takes to say,
"I wish."

My mother tells me, women forgive
fathers, husbands and sons,
even a rapist needs love.
It's what women do.

Family Trees

(A father's story)

Under the weeping willow.
Sitting eye-to-eye,
on a picnic bench.

You ask me to say,
"I'm sorry."

I study your face,
see dark caverns, not eyes,
deep hollows,
grown larger with age.

You mumble,
"This family tree is cracked."

Limbs.
Bones.
Broken.
Beatings.
Brutal.

"I'm sorry," I say

Still sitting eye-to-eye.
I pray: "Dear God,
I can't weep anymore.
Please allow me to run away,
. . . bury all of this shame."

I'll Call 911 When My Breathing Stops

The problem is I drank everything:
canned heat, sneaky Pete, embalming fluid, musky.
I stank,
was out of whack with everyone around me,
really hit the skids.
I could roll my eyeballs so far up that when I opened the lids,
only the whites of my eyes showed.
Everyone pities a blind person.
I'm too far gone. A stumblebum,
a little bit down, just a bit peeved,
a tad out of sorts, a little bit concerned.
Sugar Doodle, this is ridiculous.
I'll try journaling. Regurgitate this shit leaking out my head,
chant "there are no weeds, there are no weeds, there are no weeds,"
then find that weed and rip it out. Start a dream,
get rid of my hallucinations, memory problems, constipation,
sleeplessness. Oh, how my rusty gears screech.

Broken Cycles

He was smart
for an ordinary mutt.
Canine genius
Figured it out.
Why couldn't I?

He bit my dad
when he pulled
Butch's jaws open
threw bits of food
down his throat.

Stupid dog.
Next time he'll
shove your face
deep into your
doggie dish.

That's how it's done,
if you don't eat.

One day, Dad
took Butch for a walk,

removed
the leash. Dog
never came back.
He must have been
a goddamned genius.

Squatter's Rights

I only lost homes in my lifetime
—Richard Hugo

One day a deer
almost ate an apple
out of my palm.
But, that deer's no beggar.

I wished that deer
would come in my kitchen
and talk to me. God knows,
conversation is dull these days.

I think I'll ask my husband
why he marks territory like a deer,
but I'm too busy
eating apples
out of his palm.

These Words Will Not Change

i.

Get me out of this idea,
off this winding urban road,
this path of destruction
leads to a house
with gingham-checked curtains
a white picket fence—
where children smile, eat Slow Pokes,
wait for me at the gate.

Get me out of this idea
that I need to be a person
of substantial success
measured by things
no one really owns
anyway.

Material things, merely vacant accumulations—
A house becomes too small,
the diamond not big enough.
The idea is something you can grow into:
a moo-moo dress that fits twenty cows.

I want an idea that stays, lasts, grows,
mushrooms like the cloud of Hiroshima.

ii.

Get me out of this idea that America is just,
and capitalism rules the world,
better than socialism, communism, fascism.
America has the best government—

This huge idea constricts blood vessels in my brain,
stops me from thinking about new ways
to keep people on the streets of Detroit
from killing each other for a pair of overpriced sneakers.

Get me out of this idea that I can
make a difference in a world,
where I am a speck of dust
in a giant bowl called earth, a world larger
than I can imagine because my mind
is too limited by traditional thinking,
trapped in an orderly world,
church on Sunday, work from nine to five,
children to nourish until a clone emerges.
Duplicate ideas stand like corn in a row,
a perfectly plowed field,
thigh high by the fourth of July,
dominated by nature's laws.

iii.

Get me out of this idea that all men are created equal,
when Peruvian mountain women carry burdens
larger than they can balance, wear heavy weights
on their heads, move laundry to a blue stream,
wash daily grime from cotton covering brown bodies
in a different fashion than models on a Paris runway.

Get me out of this idea that I need a Calvin Klein suit
to wrap my curves in a way that says, "hire me,"
I'm a professional writer who wants a paycheck,
maybe some health insurance, to have my American pie,

George Washington cherries promise me truth,
America will feed me jubilant plumpness, ripe goo,
bullshit from Madison Avenue, Wall Street tycoons
want it all for themselves, and I just want a job.

Get me out of this idea that I can live off the land
like Thoreau. I need Waldo to take care of me,
give me some acres on Walden Pond. I don't look
good in stripes—can't go to jail for not paying taxes.

Get me out of this idea that I can write poems,
Beautiful sonnets like Shakespeare, words that last centuries,
through wars, famine, hatred—these words will not change.

Because I Could

The last time I saw you
I shut the door in your face.
It felt good, too.
Once you were the world to me
Now you're lint on my sweater.
Why do you keep coming back
like a dog looking for a bone?
Even the welcome mat runs away.
Your promises are wrapped in wax paper
and fall out like stale sandwiches.
I wish I would have left you sooner.
With you, bubbles didn't come out
of a kid's pipe, just a stinky smell,
a pile of rubbish like you are
inside a pot of boiling water,
hissing, spitting, rolling anger,
a pressure cooker, heat on my skin.
I want to poke you with a wooden spoon,
microwave your head, evaporate you,
trash my white wedding gown,
soil it with red wine. Make a bloody mess.
But instead, I'll close the door because I can,
and turn up the music and dance.

An Exacto Knife and a Photo Album

So tempting
To cut a circle
Around your neck
Stab the blade
Pull off your head
The next one, too
Tiny, shrunken heads
Litter the floor
Mostly smiling
Handsome
Rugged
Yet decapitated

Don't Buy Me a Promise

I feel incredibly guilty that I didn't get a haircut today,
nor go to Meijer like I promised,
to get a dozen oranges, maybe bananas,
some coffee for my morning needs.

I feel incredibly guilty that I didn't write a poem today,
nor a story or a play: like I promised,
to deliver a best-selling novel,
with words from my dreams.

I feel incredibly guilty that I can't forgive you,
nor will I ever forgive you,
or excuse your sins against my body
I won't give you absolution.

I feel incredibly guilty that I don't need you,
nor will I ever need you
to buy me a promise
or put flowers on my grave.

I feel incredibly guilty that I didn't say goodbye.
I left you standing in the rain like a cliché,
now safely in my rearview mirror.

Take a Picture

A crystal vase
found in a thrift shop
waits for a bouquet

of fresh flowers,
a bountiful bunch,
Kroger's best

Buds of beauty
cone cells vibrant
purple smells divine

But, in five days
fatigue sets in
and color fades

Daisies flop and
lilies once pink
now limp on a lip

Potency is lost
for a darkened rose
starched like a cadaver

Take a picture now
because time is sneaky
when midnight turns round

The Jamaican Woman Zigzags a Broom Behind the Corpse to Make Sure the Spirit Leaves Along with the Body

Here I am at his house with his Jamaican wife,
my Polish-speaking father, who is dying,
and wants me to have all the family photos.

First he brings the bubble-glass, oval wooden frame.
A young boy seated, in a black and white portrait,
having just received his first communion. My dad.

The Jamaican wife, with her Jamaican accent,
tells me she wants that portrait for her own.
When I ask why, she admits "it's only for the frame."

Married nine months ago, he has cancer,
she's young and greedy. She won't get that frame.
I don't want her to have it, but I don't want it either.

Next, he hands over a chalked picture
of my grandmother with whiskers on her chin.
His sweet, beloved mother. Now mine, too.

He wants me to save them, all of them.
Yellow, tattered, curled pieces of my life.
I can't save them. I don't want to save them . . .

By the time I got home, that altar-boy
barely had a pulse so I flung the frame,
broke the glass and got a broom.

Father's Two Wishes

When he died, their father had two requests.
Don't send me to hell, and
leave a bit of whisky on my lips.

The son dutifully put the whisky on
his father's lips. It didn't matter that
he had to go to a store ten miles away
to buy his father's favorite brand.
The daughters knew their brother wanted
his approval so badly, he would drive
100 miles to get Tennessee whisky, not to mention
make a stop for a bag of cotton balls
to dab the spirit on his father's lips.
His father always favored his son over the two sisters.
Now the extra whisky was two cotton balls shy of
a full bottle in the house his father called his castle.

Since the brother had granted one of the two wishes,
it was up to the sisters to deal with hell.
The girls were not sure how they'd keep their father
from going to hell. It didn't seem an easy task.
They had no connections, not even a cardinal or a priest.
Getting more information on logistics didn't interest them.
Instead, they imagined their father broiling on the devil's stick
being shoved into the inferno. That pleased the sisters.

The brother pleaded with them
insisting the father belonged in heaven,
to join the rest of his Heavenly family

The sisters dug in their heels while the brother grew more
                frustrated.
They had no clout or any higher powers.
They were not nuns, nor did they purport to be.

Besides the father was not heaven material.
As far as the sisters were concerned, their father was a demon
from hell who deserved to return to his ancestral land.
Though, truth be told, the sisters did not even believe in heaven
        or hell.
Ashes to ashes, dust to dust.

The brother threatened the sisters with a few karate chops
and kicks from his kung fu body to intimidate them.

The sisters left the father's house in a huff.
They did not want to hear the brother moan and groan
and plead and beg to have the man with dried whisky on his lips
fly to heaven with the next available angel.
The brother would have to negotiate by himself.
The sisters knew their brother would figure out who
was the good gatekeeper and who was the bad gatekeeper.
He was more suited for the job because
he had a good way of telling fabulous lies.

The brother did fulfill the whisky wish, and
one out of two requests was good enough for the sisters.

About the Author

Denise Sedman is a 69-year-old woman with bipolar disorder living in the Detroit suburbs. She's an award-winning poet and has been featured in *San Pedro River Review, New Verse News, Nassau Review,* and *Poets Reading the News.* She is anthologized in the 2017 *Nasty Women Poets* by Lost Horse Press, and *Abandon Automobile* Wayne State University Press, 2011. She holds a B.A. from Oakland University in Michigan. Learn more at denisesedman.com

www.ingramcontent.com/pod-product-compliance
Lightning Source LLC
Chambersburg PA
CBHW071115090426
42737CB00013B/2595